W0010629

UNICOI COUNTY

Mark A. Stevens

To Martha Erwin, who is my dear and beautiful friend
and whose faith in me never, ever wavers.
To my mother, Peggy Sneyd Stevens, who gave me my Unicoi County roots.
And, most especially, to my wife, Amy, who gives me strength every day.
"For there is in all the world no greater love than mine."

Copyright © 2008 by Mark A. Stevens
ISBN 978-0-7385-6715-0

Library of Congress control number: 2008933570

Published by Arcadia Publishing
Charleston SC, Chicago IL, Portsmouth NH, San Francisco CA

Printed in the United States of America

For all general information contact Arcadia Publishing at:
Telephone 843-853-2070
Fax 843-853-0044
E-mail sales@arcadiapublishing.com
For customer service and orders:
Toll-Free 1-888-313-2665

Visit us on the Internet at www.arcadiapublishing.com

ON THE FRONT COVER: The Clinchfield Railroad Depot served thousands of rail passengers over the years, but since January 16, 1998, the facility, which is listed on the National Register of Historic Places, has been home to the Col. J. F. Toney Memorial Library. In 1989, Kenneth Toney purchased the depot from CSX and donated it (and $200,000) for use as Unicoi County's public library in memory of his grandfather, one of Erwin's most notable citizens. A massive community fund-raising effort helped make that dream a reality. (Then photograph from the *Erwin Record*'s archives. Now photograph by the author.)

ON THE BACK COVER: The Clinchfield No. 1 is pictured in the Erwin yard as she waits to pull a scenic excursion train in 1969. The antique steam locomotive is now housed in the Baltimore and Ohio Railroad Museum in Baltimore, Maryland. (Photograph by Earle Walker, from the Greg Lynch collection.)

CONTENTS

Acknowledgments   vii

Introduction   ix

1.   Schools and Education   11

2.   Business and Industry   27

3.   People and Community   71

About the Author   95

ACKNOWLEDGMENTS

This book is inspired by the work of two men: Erwin historian Jim Goforth and Jerry Hilliard, who is not only the associate editor of the *Erwin Record*, but also my mentor and friend for more than 20 years. Together Jerry and Jim pulled together more than 50 photo essays for a series in the *Record* titled "Moments in Time." Comparing past and present was the idea behind their popular series, and it is the basis for Arcadia Publishing's Then & Now series. It is a pleasure to bring some of Jim and Jerry's work to this book, and it was a labor of love to seek out additional photographs and "moments in time."

I would also like to thank my staff at the *Erwin Record* for aiding in the publication of this book, especially Keith Whitson, who took some of the "now" images, helped me with research, and located box after box of old photographs and negatives in the attic of the *Erwin Record*. In fact, all the images in this book, except when noted, are from the files of the *Erwin Record*. In addition to Jerry and Keith, I would be remiss if I did not mention the rest of the *Erwin Record*'s staff: Betty Davis, Lesley Hughes, Cody Lewis, Anthony Piercy, Donna Rea, Eileen Rush, Brenda Sparks, and Dennis Swift. Their loyalty and dedication are unmatched.

A very special thank-you must be offered to Connie Denney, the former vice mayor of Erwin and my good friend. She spent many hours combing through old photographs with me and tracking down loose ends.

Gratitude is also owed to Jan Barnett, Ron Campbell, Christine Tipton, Unicoi County mayor Greg Lynch, the staff of the Col. J. F. Toney Memorial Library, the Unicoi County Historical Society, and all the wonderful people who have shared their photographs to make this book possible.

My Unicoi County roots run deep in the Limestone Cove community, and I am honored to say I am a descendant of the Sneyds, Campbells, and the generations of family members who have made their home in the shadow of the great Unaka Mountain.

Thanks to Maggie Bullwinkel of Arcadia Publishing, who must have wondered more than once if I would ever complete this project.

And, finally, thank you to each and every Unicoi Countian—no matter where you are in the world—who understands that the heritage, history, and beauty of our community belong to us all. It is up to each of us to protect, preserve, and cherish this most beautiful valley.

INTRODUCTION

Then & Now: *Unicoi County* celebrates a revered past and an optimistic present. Through the images found in this book, history and heritage merge again in reflections of what went before and what still remains.

The book's title and theme are appropriate for this community because long, long ago, when settlers came across the western mountains of North Carolina, they would have followed the winding Nolichucky River to the valley far below. Those early visitors to this place we now call home discovered a wide and spectacular valley that is still as beautiful today as it was all those years ago.

Decades later, in 1875, Unicoi County was formed—its name is a Native American word to describe the clouds that always enshroud the mountains, pouring deep shadows on the valley below.

Nearly 16 years later, the town of Erwin was chartered in Tennessee, but it was the coming of the railroad in 1909 that laid the tracks for the Erwin we know today.

Many notable books of Erwin and Unicoi County history have been published before this volume. Erwin historians Bill Cooper, Hilda Padgett, Jim Goforth, Pat Alderman, and Christine Tipton, among others, have chronicled the community's rich heritage in print. Most recently, Linda Davis March produced an excellent photo history of the county as part of Arcadia Publishing's Images of America series. Her book is a wonderful and useful companion to this volume.

Then & Now: *Unicoi County* attempts to take readers through various time periods. As its name implies, the focus of the book is the past and present, but the past may take the reader back to the beginning of the 20th century or only as far back as the mid-1980s.

With the establishment of the Clinchfield Railroad here in 1909, the town of Erwin experienced a boom. By the mid-1950s, Erwin was a bustling small Southern town with businesses such as the Unaka Stores, Draper and Darwin, Boyd DeArmond, and A. R. Brown and Company—institutions remembered fondly today. Longtime businesses like Liberty Lumber, the *Erwin Record*, and Crystal Cleaners and Ice still can be found in the historic downtown area with nearly 250 years' combined service to the community between them.

As the nation traded quaint downtowns for sprawling malls, some longtime businesses were lost to the name of progress. But by the 1980s, Unicoi County was once again in a period of renewal. The establishment of an industrial park on the south end of town brought new jobs to the area, and modern stores began to take shape along North Main Avenue. Part of this book will examine those years.

Through these photographs, we hope to wrap time and space together in a new look at Unicoi County history. Then and now, this is Unicoi County, Tennessee.

Unless otherwise noted, all "now" images were taken by the author, and all "then" images are courtesy of the *Erwin Record*.

CHAPTER 1

SCHOOLS AND EDUCATION

The history of Unicoi County records 34 named schools. Many of the original buildings are now gone, but six of those facilities remain in use today: Love Chapel, Rock Creek, Temple Hill, and Unicoi Elementary Schools; Unicoi County Middle School; and Unicoi County High School. In this photograph, the original Temple Hill School brings back memories of another time and era. (Then photograph courtesy of Martha Erwin/the Unicoi County Heritage Museum.)

In 1971, at Evans Elementary School, librarian Lucile Bogart (below) looks through the card catalog with students (from left to right) Donna Denise Rice, Tracy Bennett, Teresa Tapp, Pam Ambrose, Laurie McInturff, and Martha Huskins. Today students use a computer, not a card catalog, to access titles, and Evans is now home to Unicoi County Middle School. In the May 2008 photograph above, librarian Tommy Church and library assistant Tina Hopson work with students (from left to right) Haley Adkins, Hannah Wilson, Alexa Parsley, Tori Phillips, and Brittany Kenney. (Then photograph courtesy of Dorothy Fortune.)

It was football time in Tennessee when former Unicoi Elementary School players reunited. This photograph from 1951 (above) shows, from left to right (first row) Bill McInturff, Tom Britt, Furman Bryant, Jim Briggs, Harvey Bryant, Wayne Brummit, Jim Honeycutt, and James Hensley; (second row) Bill Ruble, Don Whitson, Homer Gardner, and Rex Fender. Tom's wife, Debbie, snapped the 2008 photograph of, from left to right, Britt, Ruble, F. Bryant, Whitson, Gardner, Fender, and H. Bryant in nearly the same spot they posed for the photograph 57 years ago. (Then photograph courtesy of Homer Gardner.)

Unicoi County's high school marching band has a stellar and award-winning history. In this photograph of the 1939–1940 Erwin High School band, members are led by drum major Bucky Updike, far right on the first row, and by director W. S. Bobbitt, far left on the second row. The Unicoi County High School band for 2007–2008 is led by drum major Guillermo Mendoza, center, and director Bradley Williams, who is not pictured. (Then photograph courtesy of the Wesley H. Parker collection.)

SCHOOLS AND EDUCATION

Parades and the Unicoi County High School marching band are a big part of Erwin's history, drawing crowds to downtown for various occasions. These photographs show two of the parades as the band passes in the same spot nearly 60 years apart. The vintage photograph below was taken by Dick Brown sometime between 1947 and 1950, and the now photograph was taken by David Thometz, a reporter with the *Erwin Record*, during a recent Veterans Day parade.

Nellie Chandler Pate was in her first year of teaching when the photograph below was taken of her third-grade class at Mountain Dale School, a one-room school in the Spivey community. In 1953, she poses with, from left to right, (first row) Verdie Belle Davis, Arnold Hensley, and Christine Edwards; (second row) Reggie Watts, Reva Joyce Blankenship, and Ray Chandler. This 2008 reunion photograph at right, taken by Nellie Pate's son, Keith Whitson, shows, from left to right behind Pate, Verdie, Reva, Arnold, Ray, and Christine. Reggie is deceased.

SCHOOLS AND EDUCATION

Today Love Chapel School is one of four elementary schools operated by Unicoi County. Over the years, consolidation brought students from the Chestoa, Coffee Ridge, and Martin Chapel Schools under the eventual guidance of Love Chapel. Ruby Ledford contributed this photograph of Love Chapel's first-grade class from 1934. The teacher was Zula Garland. Keith Whitson, a staff member of the *Erwin Record*, captured Carolyn Ledford's fourth-grade class from the 2007–2008 school year.

Rock Creek School has a long history in Erwin. William Peake contributed this photograph of Rock Creek's eighth-grade graduating class of 1940. Today the school serves kindergarten through fourth grade in a structure built in 1948. Teresa Bowman and Sherry Ingram's fourth-grade classes are shown below. Principal Steve White is at far right.

Over the years, several Unicoi County schools—Ernestville, Roseville, Shady Grove, Ennis, Flag Pond, Raven Cliff, Clearbranch, Rice Creek, Higgins Chapel, Mountain Dale, Sweetwater, and Rocky Fork—consolidated, eventually all becoming part of Temple Hill School. Geneva Mashburn supplied this 1932 photograph below of Temple Hill's fifth-, sixth-, seventh-, and eighth-grade classes. The teacher was Mertie Chandler Masters. Keith Whitson snapped the fourth-grade 2007–2008 class (above). Principal Larry Howell is at top, and teacher Eleana Sparks is at far left.

Unicoi Elementary was the site of the county's first school consolidation efforts when students were moved two miles from Sciota in 1937. Today Unicoi Elementary can trace its lineage to a number of schools—Red Fork, Dry Creek, Fagan Chapel, Marbleton, and Limestone Cove. Larna Smith provided this Unicoi photograph (below) of Ethel Howell's class from 1950–1951. Pictured above from left to right, principal Mike Lamie, teacher's assistant Patty Gibson, and teacher Janet McMilion pose with the fourth-grade class from the 2007–2008 school year.

SCHOOLS AND EDUCATION

Elm Street School closed in 1970 and consolidated with Evans Elementary, but unlike many abandoned schools, the building is still a part of everyday school life, serving as the school system's central office. Director of Schools Denise Brown, shown at far left in the photograph below, and her staff use the first and second floors of the building for office space. The photograph of the 1931 second-grade class at Elm Street is from the Clyde Holsclaw collection. The teacher is identified as a Miss Thompson.

Unicoi County High School was formed in 1916 with the purchase of Unaka Academy, which was replaced in 1929. The replacement school, shown above, served for 70 years until, in 1999, a new facility costing nearly $12 million opened. In May 2008, seniors (from left to right) Adam Buchanan, Justin Gillis, Bonnie Guinn, Justin Brummitt, Jennifer Morrow, Andrea Clark, Tiffany Duncan, Lauren Trivette, Payge Barnett, Joe Sneyd, Johnathan Kenney, and Houstin Tittle play the game of Life in front of the school. (Now photograph by Anthony Piercy/the *Erwin Record*.)

SCHOOLS AND EDUCATION

Few high school events are as anxiously awaited and as fondly remembered as the prom. In 1984, students celebrated with the theme "We've Got Tonight," and as shown in this file photograph at left from the *Erwin Record*, chose prom royalty: (from left to right) Vickie Banks, junior princess; Jan McCurry, queen; and Leslie Rice, senior princess. In 2008, the court included (from left to right) Isaac Harris, senior prince; Candace Meadows, senior princess; Skylar Barnett, king; Amanda VanHoy, queen; Cameron Miller, junior prince; and Mikayla Treadway, junior princess.

Football in the crisp fall air and homecoming create a perfect combination of school-time events. In this file photograph below, from the *Erwin Record*, the 1986 homecoming court includes (from left to right) Holli Harris, second runner-up; Saundra Slagle, queen; and Joy Wright, first runner-up. Nearly a quarter of a century later, in 2008, another group of young ladies held court: (from left to right) Carrie Fraiser, third runner-up; April Cathermine, first runner-up; Ali Schwenke, queen; Jennifer Morrow, Miss Congeniality; Candace Meadows, second runner-up; and Keesha White, fourth runner-up.

Where Love Street School once stood, children still laugh, play, and learn at the Unicoi County Family YMCA. Love Street closed in 1970 when it was consolidated with Evans Elementary. The YMCA, built in 1973, serves hundreds of residents through a variety of activities in a Christian environment. From left to right, YMCA staff members Patsy Swanger, Lisa White, Steve Flack, Sharon Shadrick, and Becky Lewis pose with young Y members Amanda White, Chance Parker, Ryan Simmons, Shelby Cade, and Kaitlynn Morrell.

For the Unicoi County High School class of 1940, a reunion is always extra special. The class first reunited in 1980 with 129 attendees. Today members meet regularly and invite members from the classes of 1939 through the 1940s, too. In a recent reunion photograph (below) are, from left to right, Harold Blankenship, A. R. Morgan, Edythe Tinker Hawkins, George Hatcher, Judy Ferguson Moss, Dorothy Shelton, Billie Marie Price Chapman, Louise Hurd, Bill Hain, Virginia Lamie Helton, Virginia Capps, George Callahan, and Fannie Mae Clark Parsley.

SCHOOLS AND EDUCATION

BUSINESS AND INDUSTRY

This remarkable aerial shot is from County Mayor Greg Lynch's collection of photographs and was taken by Earle Walker, who captured this moment in time high above Erwin in 1968. Downtown, the surrounding streets, and the Clinchfield Railroad yard are clearly visible. The Hoover Ball and Bearing Company, which had opened only a decade before, can be seen at the bottom of the photograph.

Crystal Ice, Coal, and Laundry Corporation opened on July 16, 1916, making Crystal the longest continuously operating business under the same name in Unicoi County. The photograph from the early 1930s (below) shows employees outside the original Crystal building, located on the site of today's Erwin Town Hall, which was built in 1995 at 211 North Main Avenue. Above, Erwin mayor William Donald "Brushy" Lewis (front center) is pictured outside with municipal employees (from left to right) Tiffany Riddle, Jan Day, Janice Metcalf, Randy Trivette, and Brian Hensley. (Then photograph courtesy of M. L. Phillips.)

Liberty Lumber opened in 1919 and continues today at a newly remodeled store on Gay Street. Liberty, for much of its history, operated at the corner of Main Avenue and Second Street (pictured above) where Walgreens was built in 2005. In this photograph taken in 1988, Sherry Tipton collects money for the Erwin Jaycees' Christmas shopping tour in front of Liberty. Below, Walgreens employees (from left to right) Heidi Honeycutt, Sharon Haycock, Holly Gragg, Ashley Wilson, Cary Thompson, Pam Pasternak, and Joel Troy pose for a 2008 photograph.

This photograph, taken in 1962, shows James "Lilly" Ambrose at Calhoun's Service Station, located on North Main Avenue. Lilly's son, Gary, and daughter-in-law, Janet, who supplied the photograph, think the motorcycle had been decorated for use in a parade. Today the site of Calhoun's is the location of the Medicine Shoppe, owned by pharmacist Mark Cook and his wife, Jennifer. The Cooks purchased the business in March 2006 from Jody Moore, who had operated the business there since about 1992.

Erwin native T. C. Runion selected his hometown for the location of a nuclear fuel facility. Formed by W. R. Grace and Company in 1957, the plant made fuel for America's first commercial nuclear reactor and other fuels important to America's energy future. For four decades, Nuclear Fuel Services has supplied nuclear fuel to the U.S. Navy. The company, one of Unicoi County's largest employers, also recycles stockpiled uranium to produce fuel for U.S. commercial nuclear reactors to generate electricity.

Erwin Emergency and Rescue Squad's headquarters (below) was located at this location on the corner of Nolichucky Avenue and Tucker Street until the organization dissolved in the late 1990s. Swedish-based Studsvik Corporation, which operates a nuclear waste treatment facility on T. C. Runion Road near Nuclear Fuel Services, completely remodeled the building in 2005 for its Erwin administrative offices. Studsvik employees (pictured above) are, from left to right, Karen Kerns, Teresa Keska, Grace Moore, Holly Garnett, Bob Brotemarkle, Jim Hopkins, and David Schlosser.

E. Guy Robbins operated this Ford Motor Company dealership on North Main Avenue downtown until 1958. Later the building was used for Unicoi Lanes, a popular bowling alley. After a 1997 blizzard collapsed the building, it was razed, but, in 2005, Robbins's daughter, Ruth Masters, donated the property to Unicoi County for use as a park called the Gathering Place. John Holley and Debbie Jernee married in the park's first-ever wedding on the lucky date of July 7, 2007, at 7:00 p.m.

Horace Roller opened Roller Pharmacy on July 1, 1964. More than four decades later, it remains a vibrant downtown Erwin business at 109 North Main Avenue. When it opened, the pharmacy not only had the widest selection of over-the-counter drugs around, but it also was home to a soda fountain. The 2008 staff includes, from left to right, Dorothy Tipton, Tonya Morris, Terry Roller (current owner and son of Horace, who died in 1966), Tracy Garland, Sherri Garland, and Faye Bailey.

Elizabeth Renfro, one of the original Roller Pharmacy employees when it opened for business on July 1, 1964, is shown in the photograph at left getting her counter ready for a grand-opening celebration held on August 7 and 8, 1964. Current owner Terry Roller is shown above at that same counter, which is still used to serve customers today, and just like in 1964, the store still offers free delivery. (Then photograph courtesy of Roller Pharmacy.)

The downtown Erwin view certainly has changed since 1934 as one looks to the southwest from the corner of Main Avenue and Tucker Street. Taken on September 27, 1934, the photograph below shows the lot on which Erwin's new post office would be opened for business less than two years later in 1936 (and where Plant Palace is today, pictured above). Occupants of the house seen to the right used the lot for a garden, and companies used the space for billboards. (Then photograph courtesy of James Goforth.)

Earle Walker took this photograph in 1947 of the Erwin Post Office, which opened in 1936. The boy is identified as Lawrence Nelson's nephew, Kenneth Kerns. After the post office moved up the street to a new location in 1998, Harry and Teresa Lewis purchased the building for use as Plant Palace Florist and Gifts. Much of the interior, including old post-office boxes, was preserved. Pictured below, from left to right, are Denis Thomas, Clara Dunbar, Teresa Lewis, and Harry Lewis. (Then photograph courtesy of Greg Lynch.)

Many residents have fond memories of Bantam Chef and its Sooper Dooper Burger, a half-pound burger that sold for $1.19. Above, the Bantam Chef staff posed for the *Erwin Record* in this photograph from 1976. From left to right are Joann Harris, Kay Green, Brenda McKinney, Wanda Cooper, Debbie Hensley, Edna Robbins, and manager Jack Cooper. After Bantam Chef closed, Sonic: America's Drive-In was built in 1995 at the same location and continues to tempt Unicoi Countians with tasty food.

Boyd-DeArmond opened in 1928 and closed in 1981. Nancy DeArmond Gentry's photograph (below) is from the furniture and appliance store's 25th anniversary. Pictured from left to right are Paul Donnelly, Ted Hopson, Spud Lewis, unidentified, Bill Campbell, Howard Tolley, Irene Booth, Richard Whaley, Hazel Harmon, Charlie Deaton, Retha Sproles, June Westall, Bill Masters, Ferrell Boyd, and Jack DeArmond (Nancy's father). Today Dr. Diane Campbell practices at Boyd-DeArmond's Gay Street location. Pictured above, from left to right, are Julia Bennett, Aundria English, Debbie Hughes, Emilee Lovette, Shirlene Sholes, Larissa Way, and Dr. Campbell.

George L. Carter first considered placing the headquarters for the Clinchfield Railroad in Johnson City, but, luckily for Erwin, those plans were moved a few miles down the track, setting in motion decades of prosperity for Unicoi County. The railroad's main office building—known by railroaders as the "Big Office"—was built in 1915. Later a third floor was added, and today, 93 years after it was first constructed, that same building continues to serve CSX employees.

Unicoi Countians have long been accustomed to images like this—trains at the Second Street crossings near downtown Erwin. This photograph, taken in 1968, shows the Clinchfield No. 1 as she makes her inaugural journey leading an excursion train. Ed Hatcher was the engineer. Today Clinchfield's steam engines have been replaced by massive CSX diesel engines. In 2008, officials unveiled a multi-million-dollar railroad overpass plan that will one day put an end to blocked traffic. (Then photograph courtesy of Jim Lyons.)

Now home to Stegall's Pottery and Craft Gallery, this Nolichucky Avenue building, originally owned by E. Guy Robbins, first was a bus station. The facility was later home to the Unicoi County Gas Utility District and Duncan Mechanical. Alan and Nancy Stegall moved to Erwin in 1993, and in 1996, the couple bought the building to house their handcrafted pottery. Appropriately, the Stegalls' mode of transportation is a brightly colored minibus. (Then photograph courtesy of Carolyn Fowler.)

BUSINESS AND INDUSTRY

Southern Potteries began operations in Erwin in 1916 and was one of the county's largest employers until it closed in 1957. While the company's hand-painted dishes are collected around the globe, there is a touch of irony found on Pottery Road, located behind the pottery's building. It is literally a street paved in pieces of broken pottery. It is a stark but fascinating reminder of what once was. (Then photograph courtesy of Jim Goforth. Now photograph by Lesley Hughes/the *Erwin Record*.)

Stacks of completed Blue Ridge Pottery (below) await distribution during the heyday of Southern Potteries in Erwin. From 1916 until 1957, hundreds were employed by the company, including Kathryn Sparks, one of dozens of women over the years who created the hand-painted, one-of-a-kind dishes sold at the nation's top retail outlets. Above, Kathryn is surrounded by the collectible dishes in the Unicoi County Heritage Museum's room dedicated to the pottery. (Then photograph courtesy of Sandy Lingerfelt.)

Since 1922, this stately building has brought grandeur to the corner of Main Avenue and Love Street in downtown Erwin. For nearly four decades, it was home to Hotel Erwin (later revamped as the Town House Hotel). The hotel's Rainbow Tea Room was the setting for many social affairs. In later years, the building was home to First Security Bank, the Bank of Tennessee, the Unicoi County Tourism Council, and the American Red Cross. It currently is Morrill Motors' corporate headquarters. (Then photograph courtesy of Greg Lynch.)

Over nearly 100 years, Erwin National Bank transformed its downtown offices four times, but it has always operated from facilities located at the adjacent corners of Union Street and Main Avenue. This is how the financial institution (now Mountain Commerce Bank) appeared before a remodeling effort in the 1970s expanded the offices, taking in Pugh Furniture (the former Lyric Theater), seen to the far left of the vintage photograph. In June 2008, Mountain Commerce staff members pose outside the current facility. From left to right are Sandi Stamper, Whit Whitehurst, Jessica Duncan, Tracey Foster, Janet Ambrose, Ron Tester, Chris Knight, Brenda Helton, and Kathy Hensley.

Mountain Commerce Bank traces its Erwin lineage back nearly 100 years. The Bank of Erwin was established in 1910, but its name was changed to Erwin National Bank in 1912. The newly formed and state-chartered Mountain Commerce Bank acquired Erwin National Bank on September 1, 2006. This second Erwin branch was opened on the corner of Main Avenue and Second Street in June 2008. The location has been home to several convenience stores over the years, including Main Street Market.

Earle Hendren opened Capitol Theatre at 105 North Main Avenue in 1935. The woman in the second-story window (below) awaiting the Christmas parade is Earle's wife, Maude. Earle's son, Joe, operated Capitol until his death in 2005. Today Joe's daughters, Jan Hendren Parsley and Luann Hendren, continue to run Capitol Cinemas I and II. In this 2008 photograph at right, Capitol's staff—(from left to right) Nicky Edwards, Melanie Gillenwater, Jan Hendren Parsley, Tammy Pardue, and Adam McNutt—poses with some goodies from the concession stand.

The Hendren family opened the Holiday Drive-In on Mohawk Drive in Erwin in 1953 and provided years of entertainment from the 70-foot screen. The 6-acre complex is shown at the top of this aerial shot. Today the Center on Aging and Health is located there. Pictured below are members of the center's staff; from left to right are Alex Gaddy, Debbie Wainwright, Elizabeth Berry, Rachel Hicks, Robin Davis, Alice Miller, Mickey Jordan, Elecia Lonon, Katherine Walters, Christian Cunningham, and Jean Birchfield. (Aerial photograph courtesy of Pam Banks.)

Debbie Tittle supplied the above image of her grandparents, Jesse Marshall McInturff and his wife, Julia Hannah Click McInturff, at their restaurant, the Jesse Mc Café. The popular downtown eatery was located at 115 North Main Avenue, the current location of Keesecker Appliance and Furniture. In the early spring of 1946, P. M. Keesecker bought the building and opened the store. His son and daughter-in-law, Sam and Penny (pictured below), continue to operate the business there today.

After years as Range Chevrolet and later Jim Rule Chevrolet and Don Harris Chevrolet, this building at 1414 North Main Avenue was converted into Unicoi County Gas Utility District offices. Employees initially were puzzled when customers asked things like, "Could you pop the hood and let me take a look?" Eventually, they realized customers thought the location was still a car dealership. Utility office staff members (from left to right) Melissa Ford, Shirley Stockton, Peggy Randolph, René Bailey, Kelly McNutt, and Judy Ayers are some of the utility's employees today.

A grand opening was held on November 13, 1984, for this modern shopping center (pictured below) along Erwin's North Main Avenue featuring a Revco Discount Drug and a Giant supermarket. By March 1985, however, the Giant chain had been sold to Salisbury, North Carolina–based Food Lion. The community-oriented grocery chain chose the Erwin store to undergo a coveted $2.6 million "renewal" in 2008. The Food Lion management team includes (from left to right) Walter Berry, Freda Tipton, Mark Ray, Rocky Tilson, and Andy Grill.

BUSINESS AND INDUSTRY

White's Fresh Foods began in 1946 when Robert L. "Bob" and Ruth White opened a store called Gateway Service Station and Grocery on North Main Avenue. In 1956, the couple transformed the store into White's Supermarket. In the 1960s, the Whites, now with son, Doug, as part owner, opened White's No. 2 on the south end of Erwin. In July 1978, preliminary work began on the Village Shopping Center (pictured below) with White's as the anchor store. There are now 14 White's stores throughout the region.

Ed and Leslie Engle opened Engle Esso in 1956. This photograph from 1957, when gas sold for 32¢ a gallon, shows Ed and his nephew, C. H. Engle, at the Erwin business on Jackson-Love Highway. After Ed's death in 1991, Leslie and his wife, Dale, operated the business, by then renamed Engle's Exxon, until it was sold to Ed's son, Shannon, in 2006. Today Shannon carries on the nearly lost tradition of pumping gas for customers like Kathryn Henderson of Unicoi.

Earle Walker captured this downtown Erwin photograph (below) in 1947 at the Main Avenue and Gay Street intersection and called it "the heart of Erwin." The traffic light had only recently been installed. Most of the stores—Coley's Drugs and Unaka Stores, for example—have long since closed, but Clinchfield Drug Company continues to operate from the same location. That is Kenneth "Gomer" Hensley riding his bike down Main Avenue in June 2008. (Then photograph courtesy of Greg Lynch.)

The Stancil and Ayers Grocery store (pictured below), located on the corner of Rock Creek and Norton Hollow Roads, was operated from 1953 until 1956 by Hoyal and Juanita Stancil and Juanita's sister, Mae Ayers. In the vintage photograph are, from left to right, Venton Banner, Floyd Day, Bruce "P. I." Ayers, and Hoyal Stancil. Today the building is home to David's Used Furniture and More. David's wife, Debbie Murr, is pictured in front of the store. (Then photograph courtesy of Debbie Tittle.)

BUSINESS AND INDUSTRY

The *Erwin Record* was first published on January 27, 1928. The *Record*, located at 218 Gay Street, and the *Johnson City Press*'s Erwin bureau, located at 216 Gay Street, underwent a $250,000 renovation in 1999 (the last renovation had been in 1976, pictured above). Below, staff members for both companies include, from left to right, Stanford Dailey, Mark Stevens, Jerry Hilliard, Brenda Sparks, Keith Whitson, Anthony Piercy, Cody Lewis, Eileen Rush, Dennis Swift, Betty Davis, Lesley Hughes, Quentin Carter, Jim Wozniak, and Donna Rea. (Now photograph by Adam Campbell.)

Before the *Erwin Record* expanded into the building at 220 Gay Street, several businesses had been located there, including R. C. Peterson Grocery. In this photograph from the early 1950s, (from left to right) attorney Jim Gouge, store owner R. C. "Bob" Peterson, and an unidentified gentleman check out a new product. In June 2008, Jennifer Broce, granddaughter of the newspaper's founder and first publisher Alma Broce, poses with an October 3, 1940, copy of the *Erwin Record*. (Then photograph courtesy of Charles Peterson.)

In 1997, Clinchfield Federal Credit Union (CFCU) constructed this beautiful new building where the home once owned by the Dwight Guinn family had stood on North Main Avenue. The credit union was formed as a financial cooperative for Clinchfield Railroad employees in 1947. When Sandy Lingerfelt, who serves as CFCU's chief executive officer, came to work for the credit union in 1977, there were 1,265 members and $1.6 million in assets. Today membership exceeds 6,100, and assets have reached $60 million.

Before Valley Funeral Home opened at 1085 North Main Avenue in Erwin, this building had been home to several businesses, including Free Service Tire Store; Erwin Chrysler, Plymouth, Dodge (shown below); and finally, in the 1980s, Jerry Hasty and Mike May's Erwin Van Conversion. In 1988, Sam Pate, Larry Pate, Kenneth Lewis, Tim Lewis, and Michael Peterson opened the funeral home. In 1989, ownership transferred to Peterson and the Tetrick Funeral Home company.

In the early 1980s, the Town of Erwin and Unicoi County began acquiring property for the county's first industrial park. Several major companies, including A. B. Plastics, Allstate Builders, BlueLinx, PolyPipe, Preston Tool and Mold, and Impact Plastics are now located in Riverview Industrial Park. Industrial Drive connects the park with Jackson-Love Highway and Interstate 26, and the park has access to CSX rail services. The Erwin Linear Trail winds along the park near the Nolichucky River.

PolyPipe was Riverview Industrial Park's first on-line industry when full operations began in May 1987. Nearly a year before, in June 1986, the company held a test run with a 500-foot coil of 2-inch poly gas pipe, which is shown above being reeled onto a machine in the plant. Today PolyPipe remains a cornerstone of the park and a large employer for Unicoi County.

A $430,000 state economic development grant helped bring Jerry O'Connor's Impact Plastics to Riverview Industrial Park in 1988. In this October 1988 photograph below, O'Connor, center, finalizes the grant details. He is flanked by businessman Fred Donato and accountant Barnett Rukin. Standing are county attorney David Shults, county commission chairman Russell Brackins, businessman Dennis Rocillo, and attorney Robert Arrington. Twenty years later, O'Connor still operates his custom-injector plastics company at a 17-acre site in the park and employs 107 workers.

Unicoi County Memorial Hospital opened on February 1, 1953. For its 20th anniversary, the hospital celebrated with this cake made in the shape of the hospital. Pictured below, from left to right, are (first row) Beulah Higgins, Eleanor Senter, Hazel Tipton, Pauline Robinson, and Walter Bryant; (second row) W. H. McFarland, Dr. Robert H. Harvey, and administrator Pauline Vaughn. In 2008, longtime staff members (from left to right) Paulette Edwards, Connie Miller, Pam Love, Linda Stewart, and chief executive officer Jim Pate pose outside the hospital.

Erwin Utilities, established in 1945, is the Town of Erwin's public-owned utility company, providing electricity, water, and sewer services to thousands of Unicoi County residents. Employees gathered for a photograph outside the utility's headquarters, located on Love Street. That building underwent a major overhaul in 2008 and is shown below in the new construction phase. Lee Brown is the current general manager. He succeeded his father, who served in the same position for many years.

Robert and Stanley Love began Erwin Motors in 1958 with the purchase of Robbins Motors downtown. In 1963, the dealership moved to Ohio Avenue, where this photograph (at right) was taken of (from left to right) Robert, Stanley, Dorothy Wiggand, Willie Robinson, Joe Gouge, Hubert Bailey, Dewey Tipton, George Horton, Link White, and Arnold Bailey. Today Erwin Motors is owned by Robert and Stanley's brother, Ted Love, and Ted's son, Todd, pictured below with Todd's son, Joshua, at the dealership, located on Main Avenue since 1988.

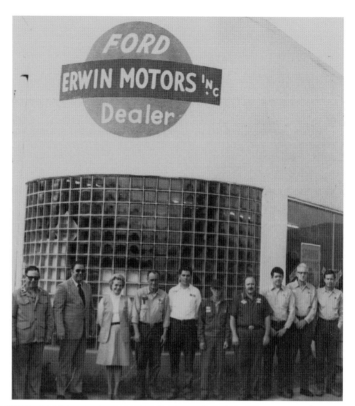

The Devil's Looking Glass is an 800-foot cliff that rises above the Nolichucky River. According to local lore, a Spanish expedition in 1566 under Juan Pardo named the majestic rock formation *el Espejo del Diablo*. The Creek Indians would later relate this name to English-speaking explorers, who translated the name to the Devil's Looking Glass. Today Dennis Nedelman's River's Edge Restaurant offers diners a chance to enjoy barbecue and home-smoked meats in full view of this natural wonder.

Outside of downtown, Erwin's main business artery stretches for nearly one mile to the northern tip of the town limits. Driving south on North Main Avenue, mountains rise up for a breathtaking view, and it is clear why Unicoi County is known as "the Valley Beautiful." Notice an interesting difference between the two pictures, the first taken in 1978 (below) and the second in 2008. The golden arches of McDonald's once highlighted the skyline, but the fast-food eatery's former building is now a Bank of Tennessee branch.

W. J. "Bill" Jones opened the Savings Center in 1964 but moved his store from Main Avenue to the corner of Gay Street and Elm Avenue. Jones billed the store, which closed in 1994, as "one long block of discount prices." Employees were well known for dress-up days, and pictured above at a 1980s Christmas are (from left to right) Florence Allen, Betty Cox, Robin Briggs (Santa), Wilma Hughes, and Gail Derrick. Since 2005, the building has been home to Liberty Lumber. (Then photograph courtesy of Betty Cox.)

This aerial shot (above) by Earle Walker was probably taken in 1968. It is an impressive look at Erwin's most southern end before major development occurred in the late 1990s. Riverview Baptist Church is visible at the far left of both photographs. Today, in an aerial shot by Dan Wilson in June 2008, the Holiday Inn Express and the Appco convenience center are both visible in an area that was once farmland. Interstate 26 is also clearly visible in the current photograph.

PEOPLE AND COMMUNITY

Bertha and Pleasey Sneyd made their home all their lives in the Limestone Cove community in Unicoi. This photograph, captured by their granddaughter, Donna White, shows them stringing beans from their gardens. Their four children, Ray Sneyd, Peggy Stevens, Geraldine Love, and Lee Sneyd, have always lived in or close by the Cove.

The Unicoi County Sheriff's Department serves and protects all of the Valley Beautiful. From 1986 to 1994, Robert Whitson (first row, third from right) was elected to serve as sheriff. Two future sheriffs would serve under Whitson—Pete DeStefano and David "Kent" Harris, who has served as sheriff since 2002. Harris is seen at far left in this above photograph, which was taken on the steps of the Unicoi County Courthouse.

PEOPLE AND COMMUNITY

Veterans of Foreign Wars Ladies Auxiliary Erwin Post No. 5809 formed in 1950 with 26 founding members. This vintage photograph shows members at the VFW Hall. Pictured above, from left to right, are Grace Cox, Virginia McInturff, Ethel Hatcher, Lucille Harris, Adeline King, two unidentified, Etta Richardson, Ruth Randolph, unidentified, Agnes Altman and unidentified. While the ladies have since given up their charter, former members (from left to right) Shirley Minor, Patsy Wimsatt, Gail Johnson, Georgia Emmert, and Dorothy Burrow still meet at the VFW Hall and honor local veterans.

Nearly 90 years have passed between these two photographs, but First Christian Church's steeple on Main Avenue is visible in both. The 1916 picture is a view of Erwin looking in a northerly direction from the area now home to Gentry Stadium, Unicoi County High School's football field. Near the stadium today is the Unicoi County Veterans Memorial Park, dedicated in October 2004. More than 5,100 names of county veterans are engraved in stone there. (Then photograph courtesy of James Goforth.)

PEOPLE AND COMMUNITY

Some time around 1940, Gladys Ayers McInturff (pictured below) posed on these steps leading to Gentry Stadium, and nearly 70 years later, her daughter, Debbie McInturff Tittle, Unicoi County's register of deeds, recreated that image, down to the polka-dot dress, at the same location. Today the steps lead first to the Unicoi County Veterans Memorial Park, and Tittle was one of the many citizens who worked tirelessly to make the park a reality. (Then photograph courtesy of Debbie McInturff Tittle.)

On June 3, 1930, an 11-foot-tall stone monument was unveiled in Erwin at Ohio and Unaka Avenues. Mrs. R. W. Brown, president of the local United Daughters of the Confederacy, had for years endeavored to erect a monument honoring Civil War and World War I veterans. During the ceremony, Mrs. Brown pinned Elbert L. Bailey, the county's only living Confederate veteran, with the Cross of Honor. He is pictured below with Mrs. Brown. The town of Erwin maintains the monument today.

Construction took place rapidly as the Holston Corporation worked to develop homes known as the "Pottery Homes" for employees of Southern Potteries. These two views are taken in a southern direction from Love Street looking toward what is today Unaka Way and Ohio Avenue. Ohio Avenue was the site of the first of many of these cottage-style homes that are still beautifully maintained today by homeowners as testaments to Erwin's rich heritage.

Just off Ohio Avenue is Holston Place, better known to many as "the Horseshoe" for its U-shaped road. The first home built there, located at the top of the U, was owned by Joseph and Mayme Mountford. The Mountfords are shown in this 1940 photograph at right with son Walter "Bud" Mountford, granddaughter Marilyn Jo Mountford, and dog Jip. Today that same house, located at 640 Holston Place, is home to Charles "Sonny" and Vivian Ledford. (Then photograph courtesy of Marilyn Jo Mountford.)

Billed as "Erwin's first planned community," the Old Farm Subdivision was created in the mid-1980s from vast farmland located in the heart of Erwin and surrounded by Mountain View Avenue and Seventh, Simmons, and Ninth Streets. In this photograph from 1988 (below), crews prepare the subdivision's Old Farm and Old Stage Roads. It was the first neighborhood in Unicoi County to have underground utilities, adding to the neighborhood's charm and beauty. Today more than two dozen homes are located in Old Farm.

John Calvin and Malinda Rice (below) moved their family from Rice Creek to Erwin in 1915 and shortly afterward built this home on Iona Street next to the brick general store they operated. Also pictured are two of the Rices' daughters, Phoebe and Dona. Tradition says John Calvin owned one of the first cars in town. The historic Rice home was recently remodeled by Lorraine Lane, pictured above with her granddaughter, Katie Donohoo. (Then photograph courtesy of Henrietta Briggs Roberts.)

PEOPLE AND COMMUNITY

Before it closed in 1969, Limestone Cove School was the heart of activity for this picturesque community in Unicoi. In this photograph, taken in the late 1950s, Will and Lillian Campbell and their daughter, Diane, pose with lifetime Limestone Cove residents Mary and Dave Sneyd in front of the school. Today the building, although modified, is still an important part of the community as the headquarters for the Limestone Cove Volunteer Fire Department. (Then photograph courtesy of Geraldine Love.)

In 1985, from left to right, Erwin's Mayor Charles W. Jones, Chief R. J. Whitson, and fire committee chairman Wayne Morris pose with Erwin's antique fire truck, known as "Old No. 1." The 1916 Ford Model T fire truck had no speedometer but was equipped with four cylinders, low and high gears, and a 30-gallon sodium acid pressure tank. In June 2008, from left to right, Chief James D. "Doc" Bailey, engineer Jason Harris, and Capt. Howard Grindstaff Jr. pose with one of the department's modern trucks.

PEOPLE AND COMMUNITY

The center of downtown Erwin has always been the Unicoi County Courthouse. The photograph from 1973 (below) captures a captivating and fleeting moment bridging the gap between then and now. A modern Unicoi County jail and courthouse annex was nearing completion when this photograph was taken in March 1973, but the stately courthouse built in 1915 was nearing its end. It was soon demolished to make room for the new courthouse, built in 1975, that is still used today.

Although the Great Depression was right around the corner, Erwin was very much a boomtown when these Kiwanians gathered in 1928 (below) to dedicate the club's welcome sign at the end of Chestoa Bridge. Today the Erwin Kiwanis Club still meets each Tuesday at noon. In 1928, the club met at Hotel Erwin; today the meeting is held at Erwin Town Hall. Eighty years later, club members gather at Kiwanis Park on South Main Avenue for another group photograph.

PEOPLE AND COMMUNITY

Erwin's Main Avenue YMCA, which began operations on January 1, 1926, was a hub of community activities. The facility featured a bowling alley, dining hall, and other amenities. Shown above looking north (and getting a touch of paint by James Bailey in 1988), the YMCA was torn down in 1997 to make room for a new Erwin Post Office—the town's first since 1936. The postal facility opened on July 25, 1998, and is shown below looking south.

For years, this area along Erwin's Union Street was nothing more than a parking lot that, during summertime, was occasionally used by the Unicoi County Produce Association as the Erwin Farmer's Market. In 1999, however, 220 Union Street became home to the Clinchfield Senior Adult Center. The center offers billiards, exercise equipment, computers, a library, meeting rooms, and more for the county's senior citizens. Staff and members pose outside the facility for this photograph below in June 2008.

In the South, it is called "putting people up for the night," and Sharon Peake has it in her blood to be a gracious hostess. In the vintage photograph below, Mary Vance Miller, Sharon's great-grandmother, is pictured at the boardinghouse she operated in the Unicoi County area of Bumpus Cove. Sharon's grandmother Vista Miller is standing, and Bertie Barnett, a granddaughter of Mary's, is seated. Today Sharon operates Second Street Bed and Breakfast in Erwin. (Then photograph courtesy of William Peake.)

An act of Congress created the Erwin National Fish Hatchery in 1894. The Unicoi County landmark opened in November 1897. Originally, fish—mostly rainbow trout—were taken from the runs and loaded for transportation aboard trains. The hatchery building as it looked in 1958 can be seen in this vintage photograph below. A similar vantage point shows the hatchery, which ships more than 10 million eggs to other hatcheries and produces about 36,000 pounds of brood stock, in 2008.

The Unicoi County Heritage Museum was once the home of the Erwin National Fish Hatchery's superintendent and his family. The Victorian-style home is more than a century old, and, as the museum, features collections of Blue Ridge Pottery, Clinchfield Railroad memorabilia, and more. The Reverend Ned Brown, shown above, served as curator from 1990 until the mid-1990s. Today's curator, Martha Erwin, pictured below with assistant curator Jack Yarber, has worked in various capacities for the museum since 1983.

Unicoi has been home to Don Wilson's family and friends for generations. Pictured in the 1950s (from left to right) are (first row) Marie McLaughlin, Jeanette Wilson, Patty Wilson, and Wanda Jordan on tricycle; (second row) Mallie Wilson, George Washington Wilson (Don's grandfather), Rhoda Wilson (grandmother), Mrs. ? Jordan, Earl Wilson, Mae Wilson, Bessie Jordan, Bernie Wilson, Guy Wilson, and Pansy Wilson. In 2008, Don and his wife, Sharlyne, pose for a photograph from the same Tennessee Street spot. (Then photograph courtesy of Don Wilson.)

PEOPLE AND COMMUNITY

It is certainly true that this Erwin family wears tradition very well. The dress and the gloves are the same. So is the hair bow. It all began with this photograph below, snapped in June 1955 of Margo Whitson (later Herndon) all decked out to celebrate her fifth birthday. Years later, her daughter, Angel Barr (later Sawyer), donned the dress again for family photographs. Most recently, Margo's granddaughter, Emily Grace Barr, shown above, looked adorable in the outfit once again. (Photographs courtesy of Billie Tipton.)

On at least two occasions, the congregation of Erwin Presbyterian Church has gathered on the front steps for a photograph. On October 26, 1941, the gathering was for the church's 50th anniversary, and more recently, especially for this book, the church gathered together on July 13, 2008. This magnificent building has served as the church's home since it was constructed in 1927 for nearly $60,000. It replaced a more traditional church structure. (Then photograph courtesy of the Reverend Steve Rembert/Erwin Presbyterian Church.)

Held the second Saturday of May, the Flag Pond Ramp Festival was first held in 1985 and stars the mountain ramp, a pungent wild leek. The Flag Pond Ruritan Club's festival draws thousands who enjoy ramps, pinto beans, fried "taters," and more. In 1988, from left to right, Charles Harris, Eddie Farmer, and Worley Silvers cook up food outside the old Flag Pond School, and in 2008, Fred Higgins, pictured below with his grandson, Preston Pierce, was the winner of the ramp-eating contest.

The Unicoi County Apple Festival is held in downtown Erwin on the first Friday and Saturday of each October. The art-and-craft festival began in 1978 in conjunction with Old Joe Clark Days, a celebration of county native Manuel D. "Old Joe" Clark, one of the nation's most celebrated bluegrass musicians. In this photograph from 1978, Clark, center, performs with his band on the courthouse's front porch. In 2007, crowds estimated in the tens of thousands line the street for the Apple Festival.

ABOUT THE AUTHOR

In the shadows of the great Stone and Unaka Mountains lies a serene valley called Limestone Cove. It is there that Mark A. Stevens traces his Unicoi County ancestry and where generations of his family have lived and continue to make their home. When Stevens was asked, in 1997, to oversee the management of the *Erwin Record*, Unicoi County's weekly newspaper, it was a welcome homecoming.

Since then, the newspaper has become one of Tennessee's most honored newspapers, receiving nearly 300 awards for excellence in journalism and advertising, as well as honors for tourism promotion and historic preservation.

In 2004, he was named one of *Presstime Magazine*'s Twenty Under Forty, a nationwide salute by the Washington, D.C.–based magazine to the newspaper industry's "rising stars."

Stevens graduated from East Tennessee State University in 1991 with a bachelor's degree in mass communications. He was the recipient of the university's John Pitman Prize for Excellence in Journalism both in 1990 and 1991—the first person ever to receive the award more than once.

Before joining the *Erwin Record*, he was employed by the *Johnson City Press* as the lifestyles editor.

He is a member of the Kiwanis Club of Erwin and the Rotary Club of Unicoi County. He is a board member of the Harmon and Mary Monroe Foundation and the Unicoi County Chamber of Commerce, serving, in the past, as president and chairman of the board. He is a former president of both the Society of Professional Journalists, Greater Tri-Cities Chapter, and the Tri-Cities Metro Advertising Federation.

He is married to the former Amy Dickeson of Jonesborough, and they have made their home in Erwin since February 2000, along with their dog, Sadie. Before that, they lived above Limestone Cove on Simerly Creek Road in the home built by Mark's paternal grandparents, Amos and Verna Stevens.

He is the son of Amos Jr. and Peggy Stevens of Hampton and is also the grandson of Pleasey Sneyd of Unicoi and the late Bertha Sneyd.

Then & Now: *Unicoi County* is his first book, but he says he has plans for more.

Across America, People are Discovering Something Wonderful. *Their Heritage.*

Arcadia Publishing is the leading local history publisher in the United States. With more than 3,000 titles in print and hundreds of new titles released every year, Arcadia has extensive specialized experience chronicling the history of communities and celebrating America's hidden stories, bringing to life the people, places, and events from the past. To discover the history of other communities across the nation, please visit:

www.arcadiapublishing.com

Customized search tools allow you to find regional history books about the town where you grew up, the cities where your friends and family live, the town where your parents met, or even that retirement spot you've been dreaming about.